Raining Cats and Dogs

CONTENTS

NATIONAL GEOGRAPHIC School Publishing
Hampton-Brown

Words with au, aw, -alk

au
aw

Look at each picture. Read the words.

Example:

y**aw**n

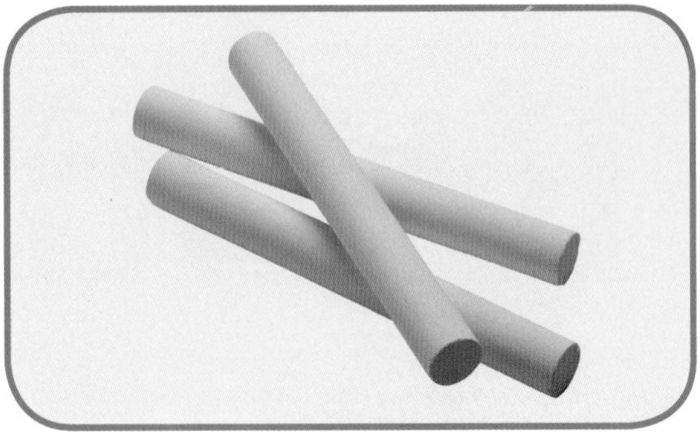

ch**alk**

s**au**ce

sh**aw**l

t**alk**

str**aw**

High Frequency Words
children
her
house
school
thought
word

Key Words

Read the sentences. Look at the picture. Answer the riddle in the last sentence.

A Rain Riddle

1. The **children** leave the **house** and go to **school**.
2. Ms. Banks greets **her** class.
3. She has **thought** of a **word** riddle.
4. "What goes up when the rain comes down?"

Phonics Games
NGReach.com

answer: umbrella

What Does It Mean?

by Hannah Cone • illustrated by Steve Björkman

Marisa yawned and got out of bed. It was time for school. She saw Mom looking out the window.

Mom said, "Take your umbrella, Marisa. It's raining cats and dogs out there!"

What did Mom mean?

"Raining cats and dogs" means there is a lot of rain.

Marisa got her umbrella. She left the house. She walked to school.

At school, Miss Jones waved a stick of chalk. She said, "Please get to your desks quick as lightning!"

What did Miss Jones mean?

"Quick as lightning" means very fast, or in a flash.

The children sat down in a hurry and got to work. At the end of the day, Miss Jones said, "Get your umbrellas, children. It's raining buckets!"

What did Miss Jones mean?

"Raining buckets" means the rain is streaming down.

Marisa and Nick waited outside for their parents. In only a few minutes, they were very wet. Nick said, "I am soaked to the bone!"

What did Nick mean?

"Soaked to the bone" means very wet.

When Marisa got home, her mom said, "Take your wet boots off quick as a wink!" Oh no! Not again. What did she mean?

What can you do as quick as a wink? ❖

Words with au, aw, -alk

Read these words.

talk	ice	caused	fault
yawn	walked	rain	lawn

Find words with **au**, **aw**, **alk** sounds. Use letters to build them.

t a l k

Talk Together

Choose words from the box to tell your partner the cause of each action.

Ice caused her to slip when she walked.

Ice ______ her to slip when she ______.

Rain ______ the ______ to grow.

Words with oo, ea

oo

Look at each picture. Read the words.

Example:

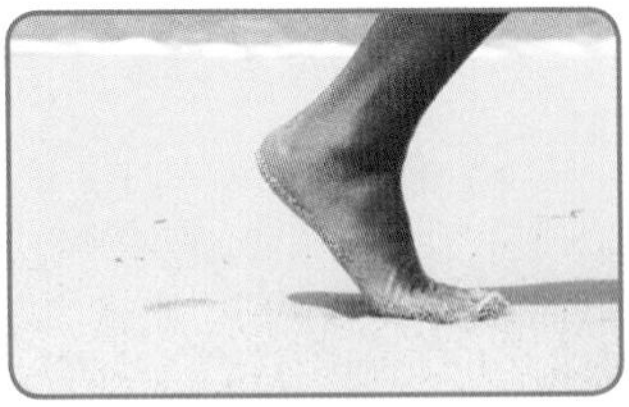

f**oo**t

br**ea**d

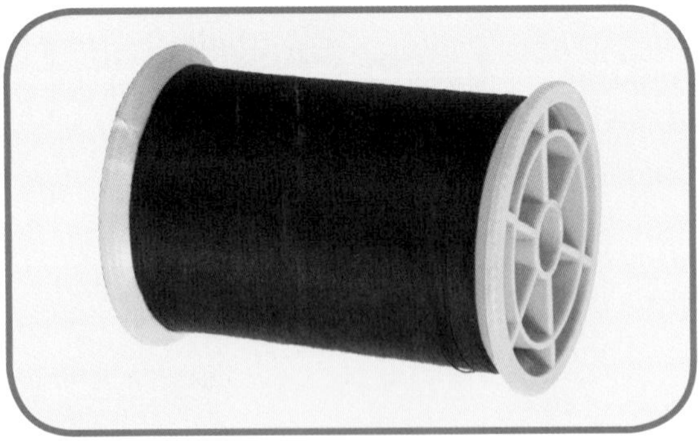

thr**ea**d

h**oo**d

br**oo**k

h**ea**d

High Frequency Words
children
her
house
school
thought
word

Key Words

Look at the pictures.

Read the sentences.

We Need Rain

1. Everyone **thought** they needed rain.
2. Then Ms. Li got rain at **her house**.
3. The **children** got rain at **school**.
4. Rain! Rain! Rain! The **word** sure sounded good.

Phonics Games

NGReach.com

Why We Need Rain

by Debbie O'Brien

Have you thought
of why we need rain?

Rain is good for everyone. Rain gives us water to drink and to wash things.

Rain is good for the Earth. Rain fills lakes and brooks.

Animals and fish live in those places. They need a steady supply of water. It comes from rain.

Rain helps plants grow. It helps trees grow in the woods. It helps crops grow in the fields.

Some places get too much rain. Heavy rains can cause an overflow of water. The rainwater spreads over the land. A house or school might be swept away by water.

rainforest in Washington

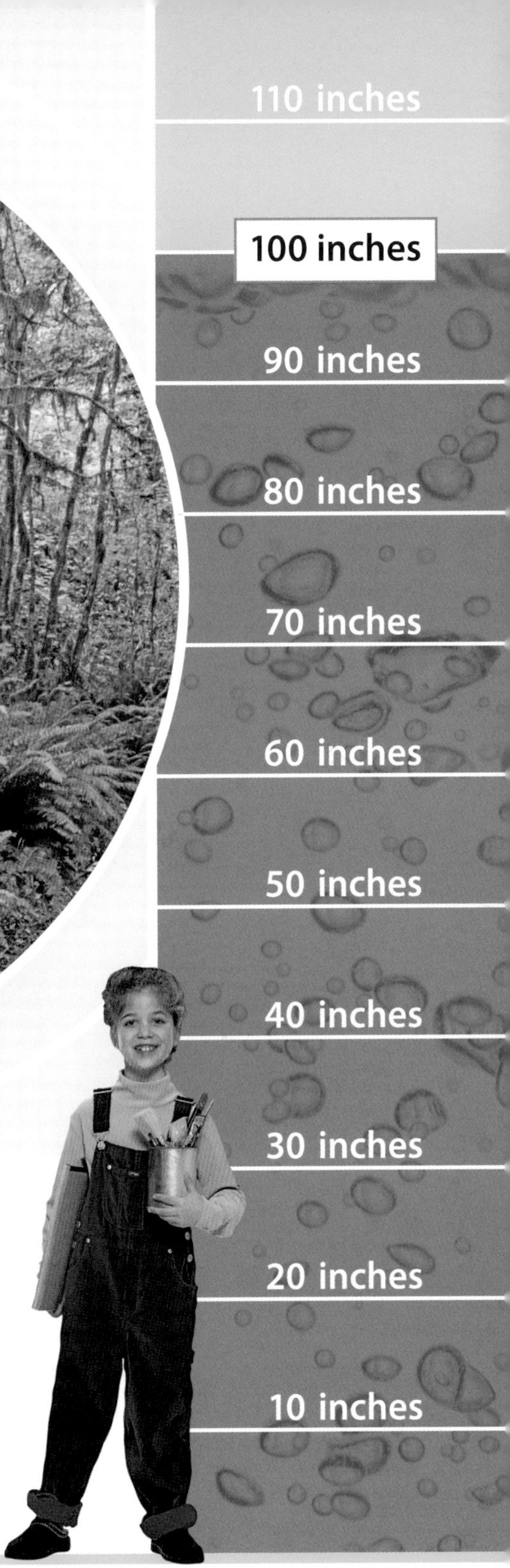

Look at this place. It gets lots of rain. It may get more than 100 inches of rain in one year.

Some places don't get much rain at all. Grown-ups and children must be ready to catch rainwater when it falls. They can save the rainwater and use it when they need it.

desert in Utah

Look at this place. It gets very little rain. It may only get a few inches of rain in one year.

So when it rains, just put on a hat or a hood. Take a deep breath . . . and be glad that it's raining! ❖

Words with **oo, ea**

Read these words.

spread	brook	good	woods
soaked	heavy	filled	mud

Find the words with the **oo** or **ea** sound. Use letters to build them.

s p r e a d

Talk Together

Choose words from the box to tell your partner what rain did.

Rain filled the brook.

1. 

2. 

3. 

Find Ann's Best Friend

Look at the picture with a partner. Take turns answering the questions. Which of the children is Ann's best friend?

1. Is it Shaun? He is yawning.

2. Is it Dawn? She is talking to her good pal.

3. Is it Tom? He is ready to lift a heavy book.

4. Is it Penny? She is drawing a roof on a house.

5. Is it Kim? She is drawing with chalk. What words did she use?

Acknowledgments
Grateful acknowledgment is given to the authors, artists, photographers, museums, publishers, and agents for permission to reprint copyrighted material. Every effort has been made to secure the appropriate permission. If any omissions have been made or if corrections are required, please contact the Publisher.

Photographic Credits
CVR (Cover) OJO Images/SuperStock. **2** (bl) Creatas Images/Jupiterimages. (br) PhotoDisc/Getty Images. (cl) PhotoDisc/Getty Images. (cr) John Neubauer/PhotoEdit. (tl) marikond/Shutterstock. (tr) Artville. **3** (b) Liz Garza Williams/Hampton-Brown/National Geographic School Publishing. (t) blue jean images/Getty Images. **13** (bl) james boulette/iStockphoto. (br) Lane Erickson/iStockphoto. (t) Liz Garza Williams/Hampton-Brown/National Geographic School Publishing. **14** (bl) DigitalStock/Corbis. (br) G.K. & Vikki Hart/Photodisc/Getty Images. (cl) Premier Edition Image Library/Superstock. (cr) Stockbyte/Getty Images. (tl) PhotoDisc/Getty Images. (tr) PhotoDisc/Getty Images. **15** (b) Liz Garza Williams/Hampton-Brown/National Geographic School Publishing. **16** Dorling Kindersley/Getty Images. **17** (b) Marilyn Nieves/iStockphoto. (c) PhotoDisc/Getty Images. (t) Margo vanLeeuwen/iStockphoto. **18** (b) NASA/Corbis. (t) Johner Images/Alamy Images. **19** (l) PhotoDreams/Alamy Images. (r) Gary Braasch/Corbis. **20** Creatas/Jupiterimages. **21** (b) Comstock/Jupiterimages. (c) Photodisc/Getty Images. (r) image 100. **22** strathroy/iStockphoto. **23** DigitalStock/Corbis. **24** (c) Ariel Skelley/Blend Images/Jupiterimages. (l) Comstock/Jupiterimages. (r) quavondo/iStockphoto. **25** (bc) Bruce Dale/National Geographic Image Collection. (bl) Craig Eisenberg/Alamy Images. (br) Lars Magnusson/iStockphoto. (t) Liz Garza Williams/Hampton-Brown/National Geographic School Publishing.

Illustrator Credits
4-12 Steve Björkman. **15** Don Tate. **21, 23** Mapping Specialists, Ltd..
26-27 Don Tate

National Geographic School Publishing
Hampton-Brown
www.NGSP.com

Printed in the USA.
Quad Graphics, Leominster, MA

ISBN: 978-0-7362-8045-7

17 18 19
10 9 8 7 6

New High Frequency **Words**
children her house school thought word

Target Sound/Spellings

Words with au, aw, -alk	**Words with oo, ea**
Selection: **What Does It Mean?** chalk saw walked yawned	**Selection:** **Why We Need Rain** breath brooks good heavy hood look ready spreads steady woods